KINGDOM
COME

Also available in this series:

KINGDOM COME

*Understanding What the Bible
Says about the Reign of God*

John Wimber

HODDER AND STOUGHTON
LONDON SYDNEY AUCKLAND TORONTO

British Library Cataloguing in Publication Data

Wimber, John
  Kingdom come.
  1. Bible. Special subjects. Christian
  doctrine. Kingdom of God
  I. Title
  231.7′2

ISBN 0 340 50421 8

KINGDOM COME

For the first twelve years of my Christian life I gave little thought to the kingdom of God. My pastors and Bible teachers had taught that the kingdom would come at the second coming of Christ and, therefore, had little significance in our lives today.

But my perspective completely changed in 1974 when I joined the staff of the Department of Church Growth at what is now called the Charles E. Fuller Institute of Evangelism and Church Growth. At Fuller I was introduced to the writings of George Eldon Ladd, especially his books *The Presence of the Future* and *Crucial Questions about the Kingdom of God*. From Dr Ladd I came to believe that the kingdom of God is, in fact, relevant to our lives today.

As I read George Ladd's books and reread

the Gospels, I realised that at the very heart of the gospel lies the kingdom of God, and that power for effective evangelism and discipleship relates directly to our understanding and experiencing the kingdom today. This revelation remains for me the most significant spiritual experience since my conversion in 1963, because thereafter I explored the practical implications of the presence of the kingdom.

In 1977 I realised there was a direct relationship between the presence of the kingdom and divine healing. As I read the Gospel I saw a pattern in Jesus' life of proclaiming the kingdom of God and healing the sick. So I began praying for the sick, seeing only limited success in the first few years. (For my complete testimony, read *Power Healing*, especially chapters 1–3.) I didn't realise how radically my practice had changed until 1981, when David Watson invited me to England to speak on the kingdom of God.

I first spoke in Bishop David Pytches' parish, at St Andrew's Anglican Church in Chorleywood, Hertfordshire. St Andrew's is attended by many upper-class English people, and could only be described as a 'properly Anglican' congregation. I ministered for two days, from Saturday morning to Sunday evening. The first morning I spoke on the relationship between the miraculous and growing churches, and that evening I spoke on healing, seeing only moderate response when I prayed over people at the end of the meeting. Their response wasn't unusual; it was all I had ever experienced, what I had come to expect. What I didn't know was that my ministry stirred up some concerns among the more conservative members of the congregation. They had never seen healings like this in their church and were not sure how to respond. By the next morning the church was buzzing about the power of God. With David Pytches' permission, I put aside concerns about the controversy and once again prayed for the sick. This time the response was remarkable, something I had never experienced before. A woman who was blind in one eye and a person confined to a wheelchair with multiple sclerosis were healed. As many as one hundred young people gave their lives to God that evening or immediately after, with many of them today in the ministry. From Chorleywood we went on to David Watson's parish, St Michael-le-Belfrey, in York. Once again we saw many healings, deliverances, and conversions. It was a colossal week, the like of which I never imagined possible!

At the end of our time in York, David Watson and a colleague of his escorted us to the train station. As we were standing in the depot, David's friend asked him, 'Well, how are you going to describe this week to the Bishop?' (I didn't know that as an Anglican priest David was required to send a written report to his Bishop when he conducted meetings in his church.) David looked at the man for a few seconds, then said, 'I don't think it will be difficult to write about what happened. I'll report, "The blind receive sight, the lame walk ... and the good news is preached to the poor".' (See Mt 11:5.) When he said those words I realised how far I had come since I was introduced to the kingdom of God back in 1974! My belief and practice had been radically changed by the kingdom of God.

Preach the Kingdom

I find my neglect of the kingdom remarkable because it is so clearly at the centre of Jesus' teaching. John the Baptist prepared the way for Jesus by preaching repentance, because, in his words, 'the kingdom of heaven was near'. (Matthew substituted the term 'kingdom of heaven' for 'kingdom of God', because he was writing to Jews; they had a reverential reluctance to use the name of God.) Jesus began his public ministry by announcing, 'The kingdom of God is near' and then describing it in detail to his followers (Mk 1:15; Mt 5:1–10). Jesus told them, 'the kingdom of God has come upon you' (Mt 12:28), and taught the mysteries of the kingdom through parables (Mt 13:11). He even used the terms 'eternal life', 'saved', and 'kingdom of God', synonymously (Mk 10:17–26).

Jesus instructed the disciples to preach the gospel to the kingdom. When he sent out the Twelve he said, 'As you go, preach this message: "The kingdom of heaven is near"' (Mt 10:7); the Seventy-two were sent out with similar instructions (Lk 10:1ff.). The apostles also taught about the kingdom of God. Paul 'boldly and without hindrance . . . preached the kingdom of God' (Acts 28:31). The kingdom was prominent in the writings of Peter, James, John, and the writer of Hebrews (2 Pet 1:11; Jas 2:5; Rev 1:6; Heb 12:28).

Clearly, Jesus and the disciples did not consign the kingdom of God to a future millennium; Jesus came to usher in the kingdom *now*, in our age.

The Old Testament

A problem arises when we ask what Jesus meant by the phrase 'kingdom of God', for he nowhere explicitly defined it. Its meaning may be discerned, however, from its common usage among first-century Jews and in terms of Jesus' total mission and conduct.

At the time of Christ, many of the Jews were hoping for a political kingdom, a military and geographic realm from which the Jews, under a descendant of David, would rule. They looked back to the time of King David as a golden age in their history, and they longed to return to that time with the promised Messiah as King. They thought a Messiah, referred to as the 'Son of Man' in Daniel 7:13–14, would usher in an eternal kingdom on earth.

The Old Testament prophets summarised this hope under the phrase 'the day of the Lord', a time in which full restoration would occur (Amos 9:14) and in which the nations would be judged (Amos 1). This was the dream of Jewish nationalism. The Jewish concept of the kingdom of God explains why the Jews tried to make Jesus king by force during the early part of his ministry; they wanted him to lead them out from Roman oppression and establish a political kingdom greater than David's (Jn 6:15).

Another popular understanding of the kingdom of God arose among the Jews during the intertestamental period (approximately 200 BC to the New Testament era). This was an adaptation of the prophets' 'day of the Lord' theory. The Jews, who went through a series of frightful persecutions during this time, lost hope in an earthly kingdom; they thought God had to destroy the evil present in this age before he could establish his kingdom. They envisaged a new world in which all evil, demons, sickness, and death would be defeated and eradicated. By dividing history into two periods – evil and good – they set their hope in the age to come.

But what did Jesus mean when he spoke of the kingdom? In part, he held both of these views. He taught that the coming of the kingdom of God involved a time of judgement of the nations, led by a descendant of David, the 'Son of Man' described in Daniel 7. Jesus frequently referred to himself as the 'Son of Man' and, in so doing his listeners knew he was claiming Messiahship:

> ... the high priest asked him, 'Are you the Christ, the Son of the Blessed One?'
> 'I am,' said Jesus. 'And you will see the

Son of Man sitting at the right hand of the Mighty One and coming on the clouds of heaven.' (Mk 14:61–62.)

By claiming to be the 'Son of Man', Jesus said the kingdom of God had come in him. The divine invader was going on record: 'I'm here. Watch out. I'm going to set everything straight. This is the beginning of the end of Satan and evil.' 'The reason the Son of God appeared', 1 John 3:8 says, 'was to destroy the devil's work.'

Jesus was sent from God, which points to the supernatural nature of the kingdom. In Revelation 21:1–2, the apostle John describes the new heaven and new earth with 'the Holy City, the new Jerusalem, coming down out of heaven from God'. This new city is the bride of Christ living in the fullness of the kingdom of God. It is a place of absolute perfection and peace in God's presence.

Because of the supernatural nature of the kingdom, we can receive it only if God gives it to us, which is why Jesus taught about the kingdom of God in parables. When the twelve asked Jesus the meaning of the parable of the sower, he said:

'The secret of the kingdom of God has been given to you. But to those on the outside everything is said in parables so that, "they may be ever seeing but never perceiving, and ever hearing but never understanding; otherwise they might turn and be forgiven!" ' (Mk 4:11–12.)

The secret of the kingdom to which Christ referred was his own presence, for through him the kingdom of God came into the world.

Dynamic Reign

Jesus overcomes evil by establishing his *reign*. 'Kingdom' is translated from the New Testament Greek word *basileia*, which implies an exercise of kingly rule or reign rather than simply establishing a geographic realm over which a king rules. So, for example, the kingdom of God shouldn't be thought of as, say, the United Kingdom, whose realm encompasses England, Scotland, Northern Ireland, Wales, and so on.

The kingdom of God is the dynamic reign or rule of God. Jesus has absolute rule in heaven. On earth, he actively and visibly exercises rule over his willing subjects and over the forces of evil. Jesus is the reign of God come to claim what is rightfully his.

A day is coming (the 'day of the Lord') when

all of creation, willingly and unwillingly, will see and acknowledge Jesus' reign. Then it will be said, 'The kingdom of the world has become the kingdom of our Lord and of his Christ, and he will reign for ever and ever' (Rev 11:15). But until then, during this age, there remains a mixture of good and evil. Christ's kingdom is present, but it is present in an evil world (Mt 13:36–43). Satan still reigns as 'prince of this world' and 'the ruler of the kingdom of the air, the spirit who is now at work in those who are disobedient' (Jn 14:30; Eph 2:2). George Ladd in *A Theology of the New Testament* writes:

> In brief, this age, which extends from creation to the Day of the Lord . . . is the age of human existence in weakness and mortality, of evil, sin, and death. The Age to Come will see the realization of all that the reign of God means, and will be the age of resurrection into eternal life in the Kingdom of God. (p.48).

We are living between the times, as it were, between the inauguration and the consummation of the kingdom of God. To again use an expression of George Ladd's, we live in 'the presence of the future'.

Words and Works

In Jesus we find the presence of the kingdom of God, the firstborn of a generation that will one day rule the universe. At the beginning of his ministry he just as easily could have announced, 'The age to come is here' as said, 'The kingdom of God is near.' The meaning would have been the same to his listeners. God had come to confront and overthrow evil and rescue people from its grip: 'For he [God] has rescued us from the dominion of darkness and brought us into the kingdom of the Son he loves . . .' (Col 1:13).

Still, evil forces seek to destroy his rule; they haven't given up their dream of world dominion. The mere presence of God's kingdom has created a violent confrontation between the old order of evil and the new order of righteousness. The confrontation is necessary for a radical change of power, and today it is still in progress. Everywhere in the New Testament one sees a great conflict between the forces of God and of good, on the one hand, and those of evil led by Satan, on the other.

This explains why Jesus did more than announce the kingdom was near; he demonstrated it by casting out demons, healing the sick, and raising the dead – all of which convinced many of his listeners that he was the presence of the kingdom, the Anointed One sent from his heavenly Father.

When Jesus drove an evil spirit out of a man at the synagogue in Capernaum, the people 'were amazed and said to each other, "What is this teaching? With authority and power he gives orders to evil spirits and they come out!"' (Lk 4:36.) Signs and wonders were Jesus' calling cards, a sure sign to the people that the kingdom of God had come: 'Jesus went throughout Galilee, teaching in their synagogues, preaching the good news of the kingdom, and healing every disease and sickness among the people' (Mt 4:23).

By combining demonstration and proclamation, Jesus left no doubt that he was the Messiah who had come to rescue people from the clutches of sin. In Matthew 12:28 Jesus claimed that his works demonstrated the presence of the kingdom of God: '... if I drive out demons by the Spirit of God, then the kingdom of God has come upon you'.

Warfare

Jesus' miracles were a foreshadowing and promise of coming universal redemption and the fullness of the kingdom. His greatest miracle was salvation – the forgiveness of sins and entrance into the benefits of the kingdom of God. But four other categories of Jesus' miracles demonstrated conclusively that Satan's power had been broken and that, consequently, the kingdom had come.

1. *Demons.* Casting out demons signalled God's invasion of the realm of Satan and Satan's final destruction (Mt 12:29). Jesus never met a demon that he liked, and he met them frequently. 'The reason the Son of God appeared', John writes, 'was to destroy the devil's work' (1 Jn 3:8). Immediately before Jesus began his public ministry, he withstood a direct satanic assault in the wilderness. Soon after his wilderness temptations, during his first sermon at Capernaum, Jesus cast out a demon from a man (Mk 1:21–28). Demonic assaults continued throughout his ministry, and Jesus won every confrontation.

2. *Disease.* When Jesus healed the sick he bore witness to a time when all suffering would cease. In the New Jerusalem, another descriptive term of the future kingdom, 'There will be no more death or mourning or crying or pain, for the old order of things has passed away' (Rev 21:4). About fifteen per cent of the verses in the Gospels involve some form of healing, underlying the significance of divine healing in

Christ's ministry. Christians in the first century saw disease as a work of Satan, a weapon of his demons, a way in which evil rules the world. When Jesus healed disease, whether demonically or physically caused, he pushed back the kingdom of Satan. What the devil did, Jesus undid.

3. *Nature*. Stilling storms pointed forward to the complete victory over the evil powers using nature to threaten the earth. Demonic forces can exert their perverted influence in nature by causing it to run amok. For instance, in Mark 4:35–41 Jesus calmed a furious squall on the Sea of Galilee, thus asserting his reign over nature itself. He saw in nature's attack the work of Satan – the desire to kill him and the disciples and thwart the advance of the kingdom of God.

4. *Death*. In raising the dead Jesus demonstrated his absolute authority over death, and that one day it would be done away with altogether (1 Cor 15:26). Unlike delivering people from evil spirits, which Christ appeared to do every time he encountered a willing person, and healing, which he did with great frequency, resuscitation was infrequent. But the miracles of resuscitation – restoring life to the dead – have enormous significance. Perhaps more than any other kind of miracle, they were

a foretaste of the age to come, clear signals to Satan that his world was being invaded and overpowered by Jesus. The Gospels record three specific and one general account of Jesus raising the dead (Mt 9:18–26; 27:52; Lk 7:11–17; Jn 11:38–44). These miracles strike Satan at his greatest point of strength and signal that his reign is broken by Christ.

Already, Not Yet

Paul makes much of the fact that Christ is seated 'at his [the Father's] right hand in the heavenly realms, far above all rule and authority, power and dominion, and every title that can be given, not only in the present age but also in the one to come' (Eph 1:20–21). Christ is now in a place of absolute authority over all authorities; he is 'the only Ruler, the King of kings and Lord of lords' (1 Tim 6:15). Yet – and this is the tension all Christians feel – evil has not been eradicated in this world.

For a time, until the day of the Lord is completed at the second coming, we must live under two kingdoms: the kingdom of Satan and the kingdom of God. Oscar Cullmann, in *Christ and Time*, compares our situation to that of the Allies in World War II after D-Day. The decisive battle of the war was fought and won by the Allies on D-Day, 6 June 1944. But the war continued and was not over until V-E Day, 8 May 1945 – eleven months later! More American lives were lost between D-Day and V-E Day than at any other time during the war. So it is with Jesus; our D-Day is Easter Sunday, and our V-E Day is the second coming. Between the two, the war wages on.

There are many battles in our war, and – like the Allies in World War II – we will win most of them. The kingdom of God comes inter- mittently, according to the Father's will. Our job is to know the will of the Father and co- operate with his work here on earth. He has a strategy, though we may not always (if ever) discern it. Our part is to pray, 'Your kingdom come, your will be done on earth as it is in heaven.' Then trust and obey. If we die trusting him, then our death contributes to fulfilling his purposes.

The kingdom is both future and present, it has been fulfilled in Christ's first coming and will be consummated in his second coming. To again quote from George Ladd, we live between the 'already and the not yet' – between Jesus' victory over sin and Satan, accomplished on the cross, and the age to come at Christ's second coming. We have the assurance of eternal life now, and we experience the benefits of the kingdom, though only in part. John Calvin, in his *Sermons on Ephesians*, put it this way:

> We must endure patiently, because God will not have us come to his kingdom with, so to speak, one leap, but will have us negotiate [cross] this world through thorns and briars, so that we shall have much trouble in getting through and we shall be in great distress.

This is why Paul prays that we may know the 'incomparably great power' that raised Jesus from the dead and seated him at the heavenly places (Eph 1:18–19). He prays that we may be equipped with kingdom power, because for a time we must do battle in an evil world.

Jesus empowered the disciples to overcome Satan. When Jesus instructed the Twelve and Seventy-two to *preach* the kingdom, he also instructed them to *demonstrate* the kingdom by performing signs and wonders. The disciples got the message; upon returning to Jesus they said, 'Lord, even the demons submit to us in your name' (Lk 10:17; see also Mt 10:8). Jesus responded, 'I saw Satan fall like lightning from heaven,' indicating that Satan was suffering great defeat. Then, reaffirming the significance of the demonstration of power over Satan, Jesus added, 'I have given you authority to trample on snakes and scorpions and to overcome all the power of the enemy; nothing will harm you' (Lk 10:18–19). Finally, he reminds them that they should rejoice not because they have power over evil spirits, but because their names are written in the book of life – because they are now under the reign of God.

Kingdom and Church

In the book of Acts we discover the early church also preached the gospel of the kingdom of God and performed signs and wonders. This shouldn't surprise us. In the great commission Jesus first asserted that 'All authority in heaven and on earth has been given to me,' then commanded that we make disciples of all nations. Finally he added, 'Surely I am with you always, to the very end of the age' (Mt 28:18–20).

He is saying to us:

1. I have all authority and power, and I am the presence of the kingdom;

2. I command you to go out in my name and make kingdom disciples;

3. I will be with you as you do this, so you have full access to my kingdom power and authority. Proclaim and demonstrate my kingdom, just as I did, and just as I trained the disciples to do.

During the forty days between his resurrection and ascension, Jesus spoke to the apostles about the kingdom of God (Acts 1:3). At Pentecost the kingdom of God created the church through the outpouring of the Holy Spirit. The church became the primary (though not the exclusive) residence of God's rule. This means the church witnesses to the kingdom, though it does not have authority in itself to build the kingdom; only God has that authority.

Nevertheless, the church is the instrument of the kingdom. As disciples we are called to proclaim and demonstrate the kingdom of God, which includes healing the sick and casting out demons. As Christ's instruments, we wage war on satanic strongholds, replacing their dominion with the kingdom of God.

Stephen and Philip, neither of whom were apostles, underscore the fact that a ministry of proclaiming and demonstrating the kingdom of God was for more than just the apostles. They both preached the gospel of the kingdom with authority and 'did great wonders and miraculous signs among the people' (Acts 6:8). Of Philip Luke says, 'When the crowds heard Philip and saw the miraculous signs he did, they all paid close attention to what he said' (Acts 8:6).

The Lord's Prayer

The Lord's Prayer is often called the Disciples' Prayer because Jesus taught it to the disciples when they asked him how to pray (Lk 11:1). Jesus intended that it be a model for daily prayer, not merely a ritual prayer. In fact, the Matthew 6 account introduces the prayer with a warning against praying in public like the hypocrites and 'babbling like pagans, for they think they will be heard because of their many words' (Mt 6:7). Our prayers are to reflect a quality of life and disposition of heart that is turned to God.

The Lord's Prayer begins by instructing us to address God as our Father. The Greek word used here is best translated 'Daddy', indicating an intimate relationship of a small child to his father. Jesus also refers to God as a Father 'in heaven' – he is seated in the place of supreme authority, at the source of power of the universe (Mt 6:9). Jesus makes two points: first, we have free access to an intimate relationship with God; second, there is no higher authority than the Father to whom to address our requests.

Then Jesus offers five petitions, five different areas to concentrate on when praying. It is the second petition that is of greatest interest to me here. Jesus says that we should pray, 'your kingdom come, your will be done on earth as it is in heaven' (Mt 6:10). Clearly Jesus is teaching us to ask the Father to establish his reign on earth, to bring the authority of heaven down to earth, and in so doing utterly and finally to defeat Satan on earth.

There are two senses in which to pray for the kingdom to come. The first is to pray for the return of Christ, a time in which he will completely eradicate evil and establish the fullness of the kingdom of God. Of this day Paul writes:

This will happen [relief to the troubled] when the Lord Jesus is revealed from heaven in blazing fire with his powerful angels. He will punish those who do not know God and do not obey the gospel of our Lord Jesus. They will be punished with everlasting destruction and shut out from the presence of the Lord and from the majesty of his power on the day he comes to be glorified in his holy people and to be marvelled at among all those who have believed (2 Thess 1:7–10).

The day of Jesus' return, referred to as the 'day of the Lord' in Amos 5:18 (and 1 Cor 5:5 and 1 Thess 5:2), will be a time of great blessing for believers. Therefore, it is also referred to as the 'day of redemption' (Eph 4:30), the 'day of God' (2 Pet 3:12), and the 'great Day' (Jude 6). In sum, it is the climax of all things, the consummation of the kingdom of God.

However, the prayer for the kingdom to come isn't confined to the second coming of Christ; it also has a present application. 'Father,' we ask, 'show us your heavenly will so we can represent you here on earth, so your reign and authority in our lives can advance and overcome Satan now.' God's kingdom comes as we hear his voice, obey him, and actively advance his cause through defeating evil and bringing people to Christ.

In the Greek, the verbs of this verse come first. This petition is literally translated: '*Let it come,* the kingdom of thee; *let it come about*, the will of thee, as in heaven also on earth.' Jesus is instructing us to be aggressive in seeking the reign and will of God. In the same chapter of Matthew he says, ' . . . seek first his kingdom . . .' (Mt 6:33). We seek the kingdom first by seeking the Father's will in prayer.

This might seem obvious, but for God to reign through us he must reign in us. Seeking the kingdom first means praying that he may be first in our hearts. And as his kingdom reigns in us, he uses us to establish his kingdom in those around us: our families, churches, workplaces, community, and nation.

The critical need for understanding and experiencing the kingdom of God came to me late one night in 1982, during a course I was teaching at Fuller Seminary. Dr Peter Kuzmic, an Assembly of God seminary professor and an expert on Christianity and Marxism, and his wife, Vlasta, were visiting from Yugoslavia. Dr Kuzmic was teaching a course at the seminary, and Vlasta had enrolled in the first session of MC510, 'The Miraculous and Church Growth'. One evening the clinic session of the course went on quite late, and by 11 p.m. Dr Kuzmic came looking for his wife. He walked into the clinic as I was answering a student's question, 'What, theologically and biblically, integrates church life and ministry?' I answered, 'The gospel of the kingdom! The King is here; he cares; he hears us.' Then we prayed, and people were healed. Dr Kuzmic was impressed. Later he told me, 'This is evidential Christianity! It's here. If we are to reach this generation in the Western world, this is the kind of Christianity we must have.'

Back in 1974 I saw the present reality of the kingdom of God, and soon after I was praying in earnest 'your kingdom come', for I was convinced that God wanted to release authority and power in the church today through preaching the word and doing the works of Jesus. The full expression of the kingdom on earth requires both – the word to illuminate and the works to illustrate. When people hear the word of God and see the works of God, they know the kingdom of God is near.

POWER EVANGELISM

Signs and Wonders Today

John Wimber with Kevin Springer

Power evangelism, signs and wonders, the gifts of the Spirit, healing and words of knowledge ... John Wimber's ministry is at the cutting edge of this radical, power-filled, new frontier of the Spirit-filled life. In *Power Evangelism*, his first book, he proclaims that God's power is waiting to be unleashed through the Holy Spirit, resulting in effective evangelism and a new depth and commitment among individual Christians. He provides a powerful new perspective on the biblical accounts of the supernatural and their application today.

Firmly grounded in the New Testament and drawing upon the writing and experience of Christians throughout the ages – from the Church fathers to his own experience – John Wimber asserts that God's supernatural miracle-working power must be released so as to be at work freely within each individual and in the Church as a whole.

JOHN WIMBER is the charismatic founding pastor of The Vineyard Fellowship in California. He lectures widely, particular in Church Growth and Signs and Wonders.

WHEN THE SPIRIT
COMES WITH POWER

Signs and Wonders
Among God's People

John White

With the growth of charismatic renewal around the world, more and more Christians are experiencing powerful phenomena: uncontrollable shaking, sudden falls during prayer, dramatic healings, prophecy and visions, unexpected weeping or laughter, encounters with demons. What are these 'signs and wonders' among God's people? Is it mass hypnosis, demonic deception or genuine revival? Has anything like this happened before in the Church?

John White's experience as a psychiatrist and as a missionary proved invaluable as he travelled the world to interview many people. His research includes the findings of a year spent with John and Carol Wimber and the Vineyard Christian Fellowship. In addition he has thoroughly studied revivals of the past, highlighting the differences and the similarities to what is happening today.

As always, *John White* remains thoroughly biblical, full of practical wisdom and remarkable insights as he comes to fresh and surprising conclusions. He is a prolific author, best known for *Eros Defiled, The Fight* and *Flirting with the World.*

COME, HOLY SPIRIT

Learning how to
Minister in Power

David Pytches

Many churches today are seeking and experiencing spiritual renewal.

David Pytches is convinced that 'the urgent need is to help churches which want to move forward in the Spirit: to show how the gifts can be integrated into ministry, providing checks and balances, to enable the Body of Christ, under the anointing of the Holy Spirit, to minister God's power in signs and wonders.'

'Get this book: it is a goldmine.'
Anglicans for Renewal

'David Pytches' book, already a very popular bestseller, will become the handbook for many.
Church of England Newspaper

'Will encourage and challenge many.'
Buzz

'Clearly comes from a great deal of pastoral experience ... the biblical basis is well developed and questions are honestly faced.'
Church Times

BISHOP DAVID PYTCHES, formerly Bishop of Chile, Bolivia and Peru, is currently vicar of St Andrew's, Chorleywood, in Hertfordshire.